Rest in the Knowing

Lynda Allen

Rest in the Knowing
By Lynda Allen

Published by:
Peace Evolutions, LLC
Post Office Box 458-51
Glen Echo, MD 20812-0458

Order books from: info@peace-evolutions.com | www.peace-evolutions.com

Copyright © 2007 Lynda Allen

All rights reserved. No part of this book may be reproduced or transmitted in any form or by any means, electronic or mechanical, including photocopying, recording, or by any information storage and retrieval system, without written permission from the author, except for brief quotations for purposes of a book review.

Printed in the United States.

Photographs by Lynda Allen
Cover design and book layout by Kent Fackenthall, www.thebuKitzone.com.

Publisher's Cataloging-in-Publication
(Provided by Quality Books, Inc.)

    Allen, Lynda.
       Rest in the knowing / Lynda Allen.
       p. cm.
       LCCN 2007925706
       ISBN-13: 978-0-9753837-6-6
       ISBN-10: 0-9753837-6-0

       1. Spiritual life--Poetry.   I. Title.

PS3601.L432R47 2007   811'.6
                              QBI07-600109

Contents

Introduction 1

one
This Small Life	5
Each Life	7
I Am at the Door	9
Elusive One	11

two
A New Place	15
The Stages of Me	17
In the Silence of Darkness	19
Show Me	21

three
The Awakening	25
Below the Surface	27
Old Ways	31
There Am I	33

four
The Way	37
In An Instant	39
Without Fear	41
Shedding My Skin	43

five
Where Do You Go?	47
The Corner of Trust and Doubt	49
The Road Ahead	51
The Leap Made	53

six
For I Am One	57
Remember	61
Rest in the Knowing	63
Weaving	65

seven
Mighty Me	69
Birth	71
Live	73
Waking World	75

To
Amy Peterson
for the first baby steps

Christine Agnellini
for the huge leaps

Ray Utz
for the love and learning

and

Jessica and Lucy
for immeasurable joy.

Introduction

Looking back over this collection of poetry I thought the order the poems are presented in might need some explaining. My logic is sometimes hard to decipher. The course of life, as you know, is not always smooth or predictable. I found that one day I would write about the absolute bliss of just being alive or the peace of knowing I am guided on my path and then the next day write about the blackness of the darkest part of my soul. Frankly, I found it confusing as I made my way through the words and emotions of this journey. As I began to piece together this collection, I realized it should attempt to honestly reflect that journey: the feeling that one day my vision was clear and, the next, the veils had fallen again to block my sight. Therefore, the poems are presented in groups of four; each a journey to a new veil being dropped with the hope that, by the end, my vision is clear.

Of course, the journey has not ended; this simply represents one small segment. I still work to see past the veils some days, but now I always remember the Joy and Grace underlying the journey.

May your road be paved with Grace,

Lynda Allen

one

This Small Life

One tiny flicker in the vastness of the universe.
One gentle breath among the winds of change.
One soft whisper above the din of millions of voices.
One simple note struck in the symphony of life.
Will anyone see?
Will anyone feel?
Will anyone hear something so small and quiet?

If you throw the tiniest grain of sand into a pond, still it makes ripples.

My tiny flicker can be seen throughout the universe by every eye.
My gentle breath helps create the winds of change.
My soft whisper is heard the world over.
My simple note can change the course of the symphony.

I will shine brightly with love.
I will breathe deeply of life.
I will whisper endlessly of peace.
I will play on in harmony.
This small life mine to create love.
This small life mine to bring peace.
This small life my gift to receive and to give.
This small life can light the way.

This small life mine to create ripples.
I throw myself into the pond.

Each Life

Each life a gift.
Each life a blessing.
Each life of value.
Each life revered.
Each life connected.
The unseen connection our strength,
And yet our weakness, when we fail to see it.

Each life precious.
Each life with a message.
Each life with a mission.
Each life my family.
Each life mine.
Each life lit from within.
Each flame lit from a bonfire.
A bonfire that lights the universe.
A bonfire that is a beacon for all.
Yet we shade our eyes from the light and choose not to see.
We close our hearts to our connection and choose not to feel.
We close our minds to remembering and choose not to recognize our family.

Each life neglected,
a tragedy for all.
Each life hated,
a blow to all.
Each life diminished,
shrinks us all.
Each life lived unloved,
takes love from us all.
Each life lived in sorrow,
pains us all.
Each life lived unremembered,
a step away from the truth for us all.
Each life lost,
a piece lost from us all.

Each light put out,
darkens us all.

Each life mine,
My responsibility
My joy
Mine to celebrate.
Each life a precious gift to me.

I treasure each life,
I reach out,
I offer love,
I offer light,
I offer thanks,
For each life.

Not one lived without hope.
Not one lived without love.
Not one lived without light.
The hope and love and light that each life can offer another.
Each life.
Starting with this small life.

I Am at the Door

I Am at the door.
I hear His knock.
Softly at first,
So I ignore it.

I Am at the door.
I hear Him call.
The sound is like nothing I've heard before.
I am mesmerized.
I do nothing, I stay frozen.

I Am at the door.
He bangs on the door now, with more force.
I peer through the peep hole and see nothing,
For He is everything.
Fear takes hold.

I Am at the door.
The bell rings incessantly.
It invades my thoughts.
I can concentrate on nothing else.
Just His call.

I Am at the door.
Finally, He calls me by name.
It is an ancient name.
A name that speaks of stars being born and dying.
A name that carries histories of mankind among its letters.
A name that pulls me, that calls me home.
My name.
I realize that only He would know it.
Fear disappears.

I Am at the door.
The barrier between us gone.
Face to face I Am.

Heart to heart I Am.
Home I Am.
Called home by the One and by all.
His gaze so loving.
His words so sure.
The mystery known to me.
Wisdom remembered.

I Am at the door.
New voices call to me now.
I go forth and learn from them.
One.

I Am at the door.
Gently pushing me back out the door.
Time for the journey to begin anew.
One final time to bring peace at last.

I Am in my heart.

Elusive One

I'm searching for something inside me.
I feel for it with my hands,
Exploring the nooks and crannies
Of my heart
Of my memories.
Still, it is elusive.

Searching without knowing
What it is I've lost.
I can't remember.
I had it,
Now it's gone.

I can almost taste it on my tongue.
I can hear its echo in my ears,
I see its reflection in my own eyes.
Yet, it is elusive.

I'm lost without it.
I spin and spin
Seeking the way,
The way out,
The way home.

I would call to it,
But I don't know its name.
I don't know what form it takes.
It is elusive.

In despair, I sit where I once stood.
I cry where I once sang.
I whimper where I once laughed.
I fall where I once flew.
Sprawled on the bottom of all there is,
I look up through my wasted tears.

There is no pity for me,
no helping hand reaching down,
no angel on the wing.
Only me, still searching.
Elusive.

In the dead silence I have reached
A whisper drifts up from depths unseen.
Looking down,
My feet are not alone.
They rest on shoulders.
The shoulders of the one I lost.

Elusive one.
He was there all along.
He stands and bears me from the depths,
His shoulders steady.

Where have you been?
My words fall from a great height now,
His struggle on tiny wings to reach me,
"I was never lost.
You forgot where to look."

On his shoulders
I reach the rim of Everywhere.
I climb up and see all.
I pull him after me.
Side by side now.
All memory restored.
The search ends
In his eyes.

two

A New Place

Why must I come back to this place that I hate?
Why must I come back here and wait?

This is the place where doubt leaves me unable to see.
This is the place where emptiness fills me.

Is this a place of my own creation?
Is this a place of my own imagination?

Why would I create such darkness and fear?
Why would I want to keep coming back here?

I can no longer take comfort in this place I know so well.
I can no longer live in my own private hell.

The joy within me is too strong to live in a place so stark.
The light within me is too strong to dwell in the dark.

Yet, I can't remember how to see when all is night.
Yet, I can't remember the way back to the light.

I do not hear the cavalry; I do not hear their call.
I do not hear guidance; I hear only my cry as I fall.

Who will appear and set me back on my feet?
Who will appear my lesson to complete?

For I can linger here no longer, it's not where I belong.
For I can linger here no longer, my faith is too strong.

I must let go of this old place that I love and I hate.
I must choose a new place where love and joy await.

The Stages of Me

I am who I was, and yet I am not.
Now I am more.
I do not dislike who I was.
I look with joy on the old me.
The choices I made then, led me to today,
To who I have become.
I do not regret my choices,
They were neither good nor bad.
Just choices.
They led me to the joy I have now.

There was no harm in who I was.
Imperfect, yes.
Though I am further down the path now,
Still I am imperfect.
Making more choices that will lead me on,
To the me I have yet to become.
Then I'll look back on me now with fondness.
Knowing that the choices I make today
Will lead me there
Lead me to become more of myself than ever before.

My gratitude grows for all the stages of me,
The old me,
The new me,
The me I sense on the horizon.

In the Silence of Darkness

I have learned the lessons of the silence.
I have learned the lessons of the darkness.
Without them, I could not stand in the light.
Without them, I could not hear the beauty in the song.

Silence holds the echoes of past and future.
It is a place of release.
It is a place of hope.
Silence brings peace.

Darkness holds the shadows of fears unfounded.
It is a place of discovery.
It is a place of recovery.
Darkness brings peace.

Only in the silence of the darkness can the pieces be found.
Only by feel can the pieces be put back together.
Only after the night can the birds awaken the dawn,
And with just their voices lift the heavy darkness.

My voice will be like that of the birds,
I will awaken the dawn.
My voice will break through the silence.
My voice will drive out the darkness.
My voice.
I sing with the power of dawn.

Show Me

I am soft, pliable clay in your fingers,
Mold me.
I am thick, vibrant pigments on your brush,
Paint with me.
I am all the notes of song,
Create a melody with me.
I am words on the tip of your tongue,
Speak me.
I am a seed waiting for nourishment,
Grow me.
I am here to do your work,
Show me.
I am love waiting to be shared,
Let it flow from me.
I am divine.

three

The Awakening

In the heart of all, I sleep.
Waiting silently for the dawn.
Resting peacefully until the light calls.
I Am ever there.

Soon I will awaken,
Soon I will be felt in the hearts of all.
My name will be on your lips.
My voice will be in your words.
My vision will be in your eyes.
My knowledge will be in your mind.
Then will you know and understand.
Then will you awaken as well.
Then will you remember.

My awakening will shake the foundations of the Earth,
   shake your beliefs,
     challenge your heart,
       bring change,
         bring light.

Your awakening will be instantaneous,
  create growth,
    inspire,
      bring love,
        release knowledge,
          open hearts,
            bring freedom.

Together
We awaken
In a time long foreseen
In a time of dire need.
Together we awaken new life.
We awaken all.
Together, we awaken
And truly live.

Below the Surface

I stand upon the edge,
Upon the edge of understanding.
It is a vast, deep sea of knowing.
Within it swims, knowledge and wisdom,
Power and order.
All these swim in the sea of understanding.
This sea knows no bounds,
Its depths are immeasurable.
Yet it is contained within a small space:
The sea of understanding lies within the heart.

Standing on the edge it looks formidable,
It looks frightening,
It looks threatening.
So first I sit and dip just my toes in understanding.
One toe at a time, I feel the warm waters of knowledge.
Slowly, I stir knowledge with my toes contemplating the meanings that swim before me.
Then, I lean and dip my fingers into understanding.
Wisdom nibbles at my fingertips.
I swirl bits of wisdom and watch them slip through my fingers.
Knowledge and wisdom may be glimpsed from the water's edge,
But not truly grasped.

I stand and look down at my reflection on the surface of understanding.
Not until then do I see it.
Knowledge, wisdom, power, order
All lie below the surface.
Upon the surface is a mere reflection of myself.
My true self lies below the surface,
Understanding.

I must immerse myself.
I must penetrate the surface and go beyond what I know,
Into what I understand.
My thoughts in order,

My fears behind me,
My power in hand,
Wisdom and knowledge in my heart
I plunge into understanding.

What I find is,
All I imagined.
All I have ever imagined,
Found in the sea of understanding.

Wisdom and knowledge don't just swim by,
Aren't just gained,
They are known.
For the sea of understanding is the place of knowing.
The order of the Universe is known,
Not in dates and times,
But known in trust.
Trust for the plan without need for dates and times.
The power of creation I hold is known.
All wisdom and knowledge of the ages is known.

In that knowing, finally
I see.
In the deepest reaches of understanding
The One lives.
Through the crystal clear waters of understanding
I see the One.
At the core of each atom of knowledge or wisdom, power or order
Is the One.
The very energy that moves the sea of understanding
Is our Oneness.

I am One.
I feel each thought and hope and fear and doubt.
I see the core of each atom throughout the universe is love.
I see peace orbiting each nucleus of love.
I see joy created by the joining of love and peace.
In that joy we are One.

At the core of all
Is love.
Around it travels peace.
From their union is born joy.
In joy we are One.
In being One we understand.

Understanding lies just below the surface.
Swim in it.

Old Ways

Let go of your old ways,
And be one with me.
Let go of your old ways,
See the connections which unite us.
Let go of your old ways,
Feel the love flowing from me to you.
Let go of your old ways,
Hear the harmony of our voices united in song.
Let go of your old ways,
Inhale the beauty surrounding you.
Let go of your old ways,
Embrace the new way.
Embrace the new way
And be free.

There Am I

Where two or more are gathered in my name,
There am I.
Where two or more are gathered to condemn my name,
There am I.

In the heart of the ones you love and
In the heart of your enemy,
There am I.
In the delicate beauty of the flower and
In the ferocity of the storm,
There am I.
In the handshake of peace and
In the earth shaking explosions of war,
There am I.
In the midst of your greatest joy and
In the midst of your deepest sorrow,
There am I.
In the outstretched hand of compassion and
In the clenched fist of hatred,
There am I.
In the brilliant light of your soul and
In the darkest shadow of your fears,
There am I.

In each leaf that buds and leaf that falls,
In each flame that purifies and flame that scars,
In each drop of rain that quenches the land and flood that ravages the earth,
In each newborn baby's cry and every person's last breath,
In each cheek turned and cheek struck,
In each thought of love and thought of hate,
In each act of creation and act of destruction,
In the light and in the shadow,
There am I.

In each moment,
Revealed in all.
There am I.

The Way

Come to the water's edge.
Fear not the current or depth
Or your reflection.
Fear not for the leaf nestled in the water's arms.
It does not fight the stream.
It twists and flips and floats
A dance of peace and surrender to the way.
The leaf knows the water.
The leaf is sure of the dance.
There is much to see on the journey.
A fish, a turtle, dancing plants, a dragonfly.
Fear the destination,
And miss the beauty of the way.
So the leaf continues twisting and turning,
Floating and dancing.
Joy in each dip or sway.
Eyes wide.
Heart open.
Carried lovingly to its destination of Grace.

In An Instant

That's all there is,
This instant.
There is no past or future.
Only this very instant.
In this instant is all eternity.
In this instant God and I are one.

I can do what I choose with this instant.
I can choose life or death.
Love or hate.
Joy or sorrow.
It is mine,
An amazing gift,
To get to choose
What to create
Each instant.

In that small eternity.
The power I wield is infinite.
Unfathomable.
I struggle to understand it.

In that moment of struggle, the instant is gone.
Irretrievable.
I lost the opportunity to create something beautiful.

In the next instant, I will not struggle.
I will just create.
I will just feel.
I will just be.
Be one with all that is.

I will choose bliss.
I will choose harmony.
I will choose love.
Every instant.

Without Fear

I wish I could be in the dark and still see,
Still breathe.
I wish I could stay under cover of darkness,
Safe and hidden.
Safe to be nothing at all.
Safe in anonymity.
No one knowing.
No one seeing.
Safe.

Safety is not mine.
The blanket is ripped from me again.
I shiver in the harsh light.
Not from the cold, for the light is warm and comforting,
My fear is being exposed.
My fear is standing in the full light of day,
As myself.
For all to see.
They call for me to do just that.
Time and again.
Part of me is glad to stand tall and true in the light.
Part of me wishes for the security, the familiarity of the darkness.
That part has lost again,
And the light bathes me.

For the last time, I feel fear leave me.
I watch her back as she walks away,
Her shoulders hunched, dejected.
I run after her, and tap her shoulder.
She turns anticipating a reunion.
I only smile and hold her for a moment,
Then release her.
She continues walking,
Her shoulders carried a bit higher,
Proud of the part she played.

Now I stand in the light, without the company of fear.
I don't know what it will be like without her,
But the light is reassuring.
Here in the dawn, I breathe freely.
Here in the light, I can see clearly.
Without fear, I find I know the way.
Without my blanket of darkness, I see who I am.
I lift my face to the light.

Shedding My Skin

I lie in the sun.
The light and heat on my skin.
It makes me itch
Makes me want to scratch it off.
To shed my skin.
I rub against a rock to peel it away.
It's natural, right?
To shed your skin.

Then why am I afraid?
Afraid of what I will look like
Naked there in the light.
Will I be different or the same?
There will be a change.
That's the process;
Growing,
Shedding the old me.

How many times must I shed
Before I get to the real me?

The snake is not afraid.
He knows it's natural
To become something new,
And yet the same.

Maybe next time it will be easier and I won't be afraid.
Maybe each time I move closer
Closer to me.

The layers are many.
What then, when the last layer is cast off?

I will become the light,
Rather than lie in it.
I will be home.
I will no longer be afraid to shed my skin.
I will no longer need it to protect me.
I will no longer need it.
I will move on.
Without my skin.

Where Do You Go?

Where do you fall, when you can fall no more?
When you're used to falling end over end.
When at last you come to rest, where do you go?
You don't even think to look up, because you forgot up existed.

Where do you crawl, when you can crawl no more?
When your knees and hands are scraped and calloused.
When finally you reach the end of the tunnel, where do you go?
You don't even think to look for the light, because you forgot light existed.

What do you cry, when you can cry no more?
When your tears have dried up and blown away.
When the rivers of tears dry up, where do you go?
You don't even think to feel joy, because you forgot joy existed.

How do you feel, when you can feel no more?
When your heart has given up and vacated this shell.
When you are empty, where do you go?
You don't even think to look for love, because you forgot love existed.

How do you live without looking up, without light, without joy, without love?
Where do you go from the darkness within?
There is only one way up, one way to light, to joy, to love.
You must remember they exist.

Remember when you held your face up to the warmth of the sun.
Remember when you basked in the glow of the light all around you.
Remember when you could laugh in sheer joy.
Remember when your heart was born of love.

Remember and lift your eyes.
Stand tall in the light.
Live in the joy.
Remember, and call your heart home.

The Corner of Trust and Doubt

I stand at the corner of Trust and Doubt.
To my right, the road rises to the crest of a hill,
I cannot see where the road goes beyond the peak.
Behind me, the road leads back the way I came,
Familiar and comfortable, yet only sadness lives down that path.

To choose the path to Trust, I must walk alone.
To choose Doubt, I walk with my demons.
I no longer fear them, for they are old friends.
They tug at my hands to pull me toward Doubt,
They laugh and say we'll do nothing but play on our way.
Yet I know that to be a lie, for these demons cannot speak Truth,
They have never been down that road.
I know clearly that behind me lie only tears and fears.

Still, the familiarity of a pain I know draws me away from what I do not know.
Great joy could lie on the road of Trust, or great pain.
I simply don't know.
I believe Trust leads to the land of Truth.
Yet I remain here in the land of Indecision.

Around me lay the bones of many who came before me.
All trapped by fear.
Their bones bleached by the sun,
That shines so brightly from the land of Truth.
By that light, I can see my doubts clearly.
I see the path that led me to this place,
To this moment,
To this choice.
But it's too bright, the light of Truth.

It reveals too much.
Now, I know why the bones lie at my feet.
They, like I, once stood here transfixed by the glare of Truth,
And the lies it illuminates.
I am paralyzed by the realization that the lies are of my own making.
I created the road that led me here.
I paved it myself with pain and isolation.
I laid the asphalt on the road of Doubt,
And trudged every mile of it reveling in what I created.

Finally, Truth intersected my path of Doubt.
As I stand now with Truth revealed before me, I turn and look back.
My shadow is there behind me, stretching backwards towards Doubt.
I feel its pull.
I see my demons lurking in it trying to keep out of the light.

The bones of my ancestors around me,
The shadow of my doubt behind me,
I take a step forward.
One step at a time, I make my way to the peak of Trust,
Not knowing what lies over the hill in the land of Truth.
Yet with each step on the path of Trust
Finding I don't need to know.

The Road Ahead

The road ahead is paved with Grace.

From here though, it looks unpaved.
From here, it looks like quicksand,
Waiting to pull me under.
From here, the road rises and falls,
Twists and turns.
I can't see around the next bend,
Can't see where to go at the fork.
The fog of doubt and confusion shrouds the road,
The air too still to drive the fog away,
The sun too distant to burn it off.
I do nothing.

Moving neither forward nor back
Not venturing into the fog
Not willing to brave the quicksand
From here I will not move.
I wither in my stillness until I am no more
My blooms dried up and blown away.

As the wind carries what is left of me above the land
I see the road.

The road ahead was straight.
The road ahead was smooth.
The road ahead was brightly lit.
The road ahead was gentle.
The road ahead was paved with Grace.
From here I can see it now.

The Leap Made

My heart aches,
But my Spirit soars.
I release my heart and follow my Spirit.

six

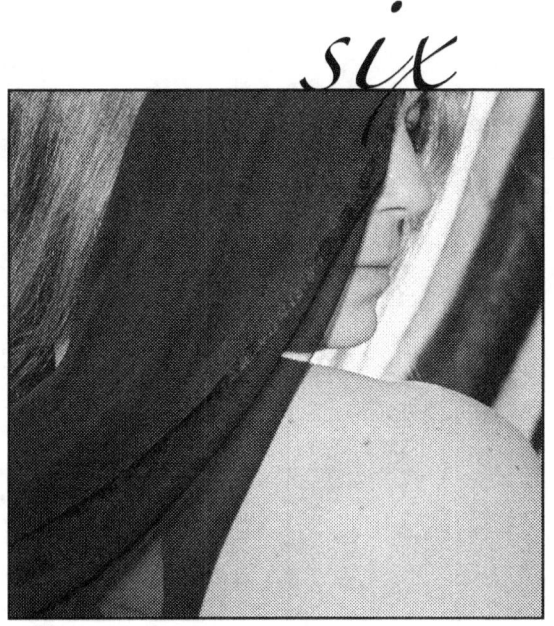

For I Am One

Today I wished to fly
And I flew,
For I am one.
I flew with the wings of the hawk.
I circled and dipped and soared in the changing sky,
For we are one.

Today I wished to float
And I floated,
For I am one.
I floated with the beauty of the snowflake.
I twirled and swirled in the icy wind,
For we are one

Today I wished to swim
And I swam,
For I am one.
I swam with the tail of the dolphin.
I jumped and played in the warm ocean waves,
For we are one.

Today I wished to rush
And I rushed,
For I am one.
I rushed with all the power of the mighty river.
I splashed and gurgled my way downstream,
For we are one.

Today I wished to run
And I ran,
For I am one.
I ran with the legs of the wild horse.
I sped over the plains with the wind in my mane,
For we are one.

Today I wished to take root
And I rooted,
For I am one.
I rooted with the knowledge and power of the oak.
I grew ever deeper into the nourishing Earth,
For we are one.

Today I wished to sing
And I sang,
For I am one.
I sang with the voice of the mockingbird.
I harmonized with the song of the wind,
For we are one.

Today I wished to burn
And I burned,
For I am one.
I burned with the purity of the fire.
I rose like the phoenix from the ashes,
For we are one.

Today I wished to laugh
And I laughed,
For I am one.
I laughed with the joy of the children.
I rolled down a hill laughing all the way,
For we are one.

Today I wished to heal
And I healed,
For I am one
I healed with the power of love.
I let love flow through me to all,
For we are one.

Today I wished to know
And I knew,
For I am one.
I knew all the wisdom of the ages.
I shared all that I knew,
For we are one.

Remember

Remember
  Remembering
    Remember
      Remembering
        Re-member
          Re-membering

        The process of putting yourself back together again.
        Fusing the pieces with white hot light.
        With the pieces in the right order, remembering is easy.
        With the pieces bonded together with light and truth,
        re-membering is easy.

        Remember me.
        Remember what has gone before.
        Remember yourself.
        Then re-member yourself.
        At the core of all that exists is love.
        Remember.

Rest in the Knowing

Rest my angel.
Rest in the knowing that we are one.
We are one with each other.
We are one with all that is,
All that has been
All that will be.

Rest your weary soul.
Rest your worry,
Your cares,
Your burden.
Rest in the knowing of love.

Rest until you are ready,
Ready to lift yourself up and live in the love.
There is time
Time to know,
To understand,
To learn.

Rest in the knowing.
Rest in the knowing.
Rest in safety.
Release will come in its own time.
Rest and be rejuvenated,
Renewed by my love.
Then walk on and carry no burden.
Carry only my love with you and it will guide you.

Rest my angel.
Rest in the knowing.

Weaving

Swift, strong hands.
Threads in vibrant colors.
Spindle moving endlessly over two, under three,
Weaving.
Weaving.

The weaver humming a long forgotten song
Its harmony woven into the fabric.
Her movements sure and steady,
Automatic, yet not thoughtless,
From memory, yet not rote.
The light in her eyes betrays her joy in her work.
One thin thread lost among the many.
Yet, she recognizes each one
Remembers when she chose to add it to the pattern.
Why she chose it.
What purpose it served.

She smiles at the memory.
Each chosen deliberately.
Hands constantly in motion.
The sound of thread upon thread.
She pulls each one tight, so the fabric will be strong.

Standing at the loom, all you see are the colors flashing by.
Stepping back takes your breath away.
Each strand part of a pattern,
Woven into the fabric of the universal story.
Hundreds of yards of history trailing on the floor.
The story laid out for all to see.
Woven with care, one thread at a time.

seven

Mighty Me

I feel small.
Tiny.
Miniscule.
Yet, I know I am **mighty**!

My dreams are **big**.
My manifestation of those dreams is small.
I'm afraid of being small.
When I'm afraid, I feel small,
   There is weight pressing on me
     Shrinking me.

I'm just a child; it's too heavy for me.
Someone must help me carry it.
My dreams are too **huge**.
How can one small person carry them,
   Let alone make them real?
But I can't put them down
They are who I am, why I am.

If I can dream **big**,
   If I can see where I'm going,
Why do I feel so small and incapable?
When I know I'm neither.

Who is holding me back when I would run forward?
Who would trip me and laugh and say,
   "See, I told you, you would never make it"?

Let me go, whoever you are;
I must grow.
I must carry what is mine to carry.
I AM strong.
I AM mighty.
I AM still scared,
   but I will not be stopped by it.

Look me in the eye and show yourself.

Mini me.
I would hold myself back.
I would say I'm small and weak.
I would cower and run from what I know.
I would stay still, rather than run forward.
I would shrink myself.

I would before,
    But I won't any longer.
I honor that tiny me,
    But I can no longer live with her.
I release her with hope and love and strength.
Fear remains, yes
    But I look it in the eye.
It is not me,
    Only a shadow of me.
I stand tall, the weight lifted,
    The burden light.
For it is no longer a burden at all,
    But a blessing.
My dreams, no longer things imagined,
    But a life lived.
Mighty Me.

Birth

I carried it in my womb
Giving birth to it in a new time.
A fertile time.
A time of opportunity.
Yet I'm reluctant to let it go,
To let it make its own way.
I fear for it in this world so full of sorrow.
But it walks on its own strong legs
Never crawling first.
It is part of me, but I must let it go.
It knows its path.
It knows what it must do.
It must touch each person
One by one
So that they may in turn give birth.
Give birth to a new way of thinking.
A new way of living.
A new way of being.
Yet it's an ancient way.
It is not a new idea.
It is not a new baby,
But an old soul.

As each person's heart is touched
They will feel its warmth.
They may not recognize it at first,
Since it's been so long since they've seen it,
Or felt it.
They may even fear it at first,
Shrink from it,
But it will find a way to reach them.
Every one.

And their fear will fall away.
They will have no memory of it.
Only life in the light.
That is all that will matter.

They may wonder who brought it to them.
What was the name of the one who passed this way?
Its name is love.
We each carry it in the womb of our hearts.
Let it be born in you.

Live

Live each day as if it were your first.
See life not through the jaded eyes of experience,
But through the new eyes of the child.
Become aware of the wonder in each moment.
Breathe in the miracle of life.
Touch a flower petal as if you've never felt one before.
Laugh as if you've just discovered you could.
Run without fear of scraped knees.
Weep tears of grief for the release found in them.
Cry tears of joy at the glory all around you.
Listen to the coo of a baby and hear the future in it.
Love with abandon and without limits as if your heart had never been rent.
Sing with the voice of angels and make up your own words.
Fly with the wings of the eagle with no fear of falling.
Play with gusto without thought of winning or losing.
Plant seeds for the wonder of watching them grow.
Hold another's hand with the trust found in a child's tender grip.
Learn the wisdom of the ages with gratitude and awe.
Give freely without thought of lack.
Receive gratefully without thought of more.
Look at yourself and see only joy.
Live completely, drinking the ecstasy of life.

Waking World

From sleeping I burst
Soul first,
 into a waking world.

Dawn rises in the east
My soul is released,
 into a waking world.

A note of joy
My soul's song an envoy
 into a waking world.

Softly I speak
Letting the words of my soul sneak,
 into a waking world.

Love the gift
My soul sets adrift,
 into a waking world.

Peace I bring,
As my soul takes wing,
 into a waking world.

No longer concealed
To my soul all divinity revealed,
 in a waking world.

Other tools for peace from Peace Evolutions, LLC:

Peace and Forgiveness
by Jefferson Glassie
ISBN 0-9753837-0-1, 112 pages, $14.95
This life is our perfection, says the author. Who could imagine any heaven more perfect than this earth, with butterflies, snowflakes, and mountain tops? Though we are all peace and love, man has fears that cause war, anger, hate, and everything that isn't love. Letting go of fear – forgiving - brings peace. If we learn this, we can change the world.

Also available:
Double Audio CD read by the author
ISBN 0-9753837-1-X, $14.95

Poems of Peace and Forgiveness
by Jefferson Glassie
ISBN 0-9753837-2-8, 72 pages, $12.95
With photographs by the author
This book captures the concepts from Glassie's book, Peace and Forgiveness. These beautiful poems explain there's no right or wrong, no evil or sin, in the Universe. Everything that's not love is just based on fear. Glassie teaches the lessons of forgiveness that can lead to peace of mind, and peace in our society. We are all one, in perfection.

Fonging for the Soul
by Erasmus Caffery
ISBN 0-9753837-3-6, 78 pages, $14.95
Gathering with others, tapping on an oven rack attached to strings tied to fingers that are stuck in your ears, listening to primal sounds. Fonging brings us to together in laughter, and is much more sane than war. This book explains how to fong. It's very simple and you can do it with anyone. By understanding the simultaneous silliness and splendor of life, we learn to create a better and more peaceful world through inanity. With many helpful illustrations, because you'll need them.

Songs of Peace and Forgiveness
ISBN 0-9753837-4-4, $16.98
Featuring original and public domain songs by Gaye Adegbalola, Scott Ainslie, Roddy Barnes, Eleanor Ellis (on a Bill Ellis song), Andra Faye and the Mighty Good Men, Grant Dermody and Frank Fotusky, Allen Holmes and Alison Radcliffe, Kelley Hunt (on a Jim Ritchey song), Ray Kaminsky, Mark Kinniburgh, MSG – The Acoustic Blues Trio, Jesse Palidofsky, and Alex Radus. The most unique blues CD you've ever heard. It will make your heart soar. Proceeds go to help preserve the famous "Barbershop" in Washington, DC run by the Archie Edwards Blues Heritage Foundation, winner of The Blues Foundation's 2005 Keeping The Blues Alive (KBA) Award.

My Love Affair with an Island:
The History of the Jefferson Islands Club and St. Catherine's Island
by Jefferson Glassie
ISBN 0-9753837-5-2, 128 pages, $20.00
With photographs
This book tells the history of the famous Jefferson Islands Club, called the "Playground of Presidents," which was the private island retreat for Presidents including Franklin Roosevelt and Harry Truman as well as many Senators and Congressmen. With many humorous anecdotes and comments, Glassie recounts the history of both Poplar Islands where the Club was initially located and St. Catherine's Island, mixing in tales of politicians and watermen, along with the harm caused by erosion and the gradual degradation of the health of the Bay.

ORDER FORM

Fax orders to (301) 263-9280 with completed order form.
Email orders by logging on to www.peace-evolutions.com
Telephone orders by calling (301) 263-9282.
Postal orders may be sent to: **Peace Evolutions, LLC**
P.O. Box 458-31, Glen Echo, MD 20812-0458

Please send the following:

Peace and Forgiveness, book	$14.95 each	quantity: _____
Peace and Forgiveness, audio CD	$14.95 each	quantity: _____
Poems of Peace and Forgiveness, book	$12.95 each	quantity: _____
Songs of Peace and Forgiveness, CD	$16.98 each	quantity: _____
Fonging for the Soul	$14.95 each	quantity: _____
My Love Affair With An Island	$20.00 each	quantity: _____
Rest in the Knowing	$15.00 each	quantity: _____

We will honor all requests for full refund on returned items.

Please send more free information on:
❏ presentations   ❏ other publications and information

Name: _____
Address: _____
City: _____ State: _____ Zip: _____
Telephone: _____
Email address: _____

Sales tax: Please add 5.00% for products shipped to Maryland addresses.

Shipping and handling:
United States: $5.00 for first book/CD and $2.00 for each additional item.
International: $7.00 for first book and $5.00 for each additional item.

Payment:
❏ Check   or   Credit Card
❏ Visa ❏ Master Card ❏ Discover ❏ American Express

Card number: _____ Exp. Date: _____
Name on Card: _____

www.ingramcontent.com/pod-product-compliance
Lightning Source LLC
Chambersburg PA
CBHW071838290426
44109CB00017B/1851